I0698260

introducción

it's important to be aware of certain cultural differences and nuances that can impact your relationship. That's why we're going to explore 10 key topics that you should keep in mind when trying to court a Latina woman.

Firstly, it's essential to understand that family is incredibly important in Latino culture. Taking an interest in her family and showing respect for her traditions and customs can go a long way in winning her heart. Additionally, demonstrating your own commitment to family values can be a major plus.

Secondly, communication is key. Latinas are often known for their passion and emotional expressiveness, and being able to effectively communicate with her in her native language can make all the difference. Consider taking a Spanish class or finding other ways to improve your language skills.

Finally, it's important to show genuine interest in her culture and heritage. Whether it's trying new foods, attending cultural events, or simply learning more about the history and traditions of her country, taking an active interest in her culture can help build a strong connection between the two of you. By keeping these 10 topics in mind, you'll be well on your way to successfully courting a Latina woman.

Learn about Latin culture."

Learn about Latin culture: Research and learn about the culture, traditions, and customs of Latin countries. This can help you better understand the person you're interested in and create a common cultural bond.

Learning about Latin culture can be a great way to connect with people who are from Latin America or who identify with Latin culture. Latin America includes a diverse range of countries, each with their own unique customs, traditions, and beliefs. By taking the time to learn about these differences, you can gain a better understanding of the people around you and build meaningful relationships.

One of the most important things to understand about Latin culture is the emphasis on family and community. Family is often considered the most important aspect of life, and many traditions and celebrations are centered around family gatherings. For example, in many Latin American countries, Christmas is celebrated with a big family dinner and presents are exchanged at midnight. Another important aspect of Latin culture is the importance placed on religion. Many people in Latin America are Catholic, and religious celebrations and traditions are an important part of daily life.

Latin American cuisine is another important aspect of the culture that is worth exploring. Each country has its own unique dishes and ingredients, but there are also common elements such as rice, beans, and spices. Some popular dishes include tacos and enchiladas from Mexico, ceviche from Peru, and empanadas from Argentina.

Finally, it is important to be aware of the historical and political context of Latin America. Many countries in the region have experienced colonization and oppression, and this has shaped their culture and identity. Learning about these issues can help you gain a better understanding of the challenges that many Latin Americans face and the resilience and strength of their communities.

By taking the time to learn about Latin culture, you can create a common cultural bond with people who are from or identify with Latin America. This can be especially important in a world that is becoming increasingly diverse and interconnected. By understanding the values and beliefs that are important to Latin Americans, you can avoid cultural misunderstandings and build stronger relationships.

One way to learn about Latin culture is to immerse yourself in the music, movies, and literature of the region. There are many great Latin American artists and writers to explore, such as Gabriel Garcia Marquez, Frida Kahlo, and Celia Cruz. Another way to learn is by participating in cultural events and celebrations, such as Cinco de Mayo, Dia de los Muertos, or Carnival. These events can give you a taste of the vibrant and colorful culture of Latin America.

Finally, it is important to approach learning about Latin culture with an open mind and a willingness to learn. It can be easy to fall into stereotypes or generalizations, but by taking the time to understand the diversity and complexity of the culture, you can build deeper and more meaningful relationships with the people around you.

In conclusion, learning about Latin culture can be a great way to connect with people and build cultural bonds. By exploring the traditions, values, and beliefs that are important to Latin Americans, you can gain a better understanding of their experiences and perspectives. This understanding can help you avoid cultural misunderstandings and build stronger relationships.

"Be kind and respectful.

Be kind and respectful: Latina women highly value education and respect. Be kind, respectful, and courteous at all times, and show genuine interest in her as a person.

If you're interested in dating a Latina woman, it's important to understand and respect the values that are important to her. One of the most important things to remember is to be kind, respectful, and courteous at all times. This means treating her with dignity and respect, and being mindful of her feelings and emotions.

Latina women place a high value on education, and it's important to show an interest in her intellectual pursuits. This could mean asking her about her career or education goals, or simply engaging in thoughtful conversation about current events or topics of mutual interest. By showing that you value her intelligence and education, you will demonstrate that you respect her as a person and as a partner.

It's also important to be mindful of cultural differences and to show respect for her heritage. Latina women come from diverse backgrounds and cultures, and it's important to learn about and appreciate these differences. This could mean learning about her family traditions or favorite Latin American dishes, or simply showing an interest in the music and art that are important to her.

Finally, it's important to approach the relationship with an open mind and a willingness to learn. Latina women have a rich cultural heritage and can bring a unique perspective to any relationship. By being open to new experiences and ideas, you can create a deeper and more meaningful connection with your partner.

Another important thing to remember is to avoid making assumptions or stereotypes about Latina women. It's important to treat each person as an individual, rather than making assumptions based on their race or ethnicity. By taking the time to get to know your partner and learning about their values and beliefs, you can build a relationship based on mutual respect and understanding.

In summary, if you're interested in dating a Latina woman, it's important to be kind, respectful, and courteous at all times. Show an interest in her education and intellectual pursuits, be mindful of cultural differences, and avoid making assumptions or stereotypes. By approaching the relationship with an open mind and a willingness to learn, you can build a meaningful connection with your partner and create a lasting and fulfilling relationship.

stand that Spanish is spoken in many different countries, each with their own regional dialects and slang. For the purposes of this guide, we'll focus on some general terms that are widely used across the Spanish-speaking world.

Greetings: When meeting someone, it's common to say "hola" (hello) or "buenos días" (good morning) if it's before noon. In the afternoon, you can use "buenas tardes" (good afternoon) and in the evening, "buenas noches" (good night).

Introductions: To introduce yourself, you can say "me llamo" followed by your name. To ask someone their name, use "¿cómo te llamas?" (what's your name?). You can also use "encantado/a" (nice to meet you) or "mucho gusto" (pleased to meet you) to express your pleasure at making someone's acquaintance.

Basic conversation: Here are some phrases that can be helpful for basic conversation:

"¿Cómo estás?" (how are you?)

"Estoy bien, gracias" (I'm well, thank you)

"¿Qué tal?" (what's up?)

"No entiendo" (I don't understand)

"¿Hablas inglés?" (do you speak English?)

Flirting: If you want to show a Latina woman that you're interested in her, here are some romantic phrases you can use:

"Eres hermosa" (you're beautiful)

"Me gustas mucho" (I really like you)

"Te quiero" (I love you, but be careful using this one too soon!)

"No puedo dejar de pensar en ti" (I can't stop thinking about you)

Food and drink: Latin American cuisine is famous around the world, so it's important to know some basic terms for ordering food and drinks. Here are some examples:

"Quiero una cerveza" (I want a beer)

"Me gustaría pedir un plato de tacos" (I'd like to order a plate of tacos)

"¿Tienen menú en inglés?" (do you have an English menu?)

"La cuenta, por favor" (the check, please)

Of course, this is just a small sample of the many words and phrases you can learn in Spanish. But by showing a willingness to learn and communicate in your partner's native language, you'll be demonstrating a romantic and respectful gesture that can go a long way in building a strong relationship. Good luck!

"Be passionate and expressive."

Be passionate and expressive: Latinos like to express their emotions and feelings. Be passionate and express your feelings in an authentic and genuine way.

If you want to seduce a woman, it's important to show your passion and express your feelings in an authentic and genuine way. This is especially true for Latino men, who are known for their expressive nature.

To win a woman's heart, you need to be willing to open up and share your emotions with her. Don't be afraid to show your vulnerability, as this can be a powerful way to connect with her on a deeper level.

When expressing your feelings, it's important to be sincere and honest. Don't try to put on a show or pretend to be someone you're not. Instead, be true to yourself and let your genuine emotions shine through.

One way to express your passion and emotions is through your words. Use romantic language to tell her how you feel, and be specific about the things you love about her. For example, you might say something like:

"I can't stop thinking about you. Your smile lights up my world and your laugh is music to my ears. I feel so lucky to have you in my life."

Another way to show your passion is through your actions. Plan romantic dates and surprise her with thoughtful gestures, like sending her flowers or leaving her love notes.

Above all, remember to be yourself and let your true personality shine through. When you're genuine and authentic, you'll attract the right kind of woman who will appreciate and reciprocate your passion and emotions.

share your interests

Share your interests: Share your interests with her and show your enthusiasm for the things you're passionate about. This can be an effective way to create a bond and find common ground.

Sharing your interests with a woman and showing your enthusiasm for the things that you're passionate about can be an effective way to build a connection and find common ground. When you talk about your interests, you reveal a part of yourself that can be intriguing and attractive to a woman. In this way, you can create a deeper connection with her and potentially even find a shared passion that you can explore together.

To begin, think about the things that you're most passionate about and that define you as a person. This could be anything from a favorite hobby or sport to a career aspiration or creative pursuit. Once you've identified your interests, start sharing them with the woman you're interested in.

Continuing on the topic of sharing your interests with a woman to seduce her, another effective strategy is to invite her to participate in your hobbies or activities. This can be a great way to bond and create shared experiences that can deepen your connection.

For example, if you're a sports fan, invite her to watch a game with you or take her to a game in person. Show her your favorite team and players and explain the rules of the game. You could also teach her how to play a sport or activity that you enjoy, such as golf, tennis, or chess.

Or if you're into art or culture, take her to a museum or art exhibit and share your knowledge and appreciation for the art. You could also introduce her to your favorite authors, filmmakers, or musicians and discuss your thoughts and feelings about their work.

By inviting her to participate in your interests and activities, you can also learn more about her and her passions. Ask her questions about what she enjoys and what drives her. Listen attentively and show a genuine interest in what she has to say.

Remember, the goal is not to convert her into a carbon copy of yourself. Instead, it's about creating shared experiences and finding common ground that can deepen your connection and build a foundation for a meaningful relationship.

In conclusion, sharing your interests with a woman can be a powerful way to create a connection and find common ground. By inviting her to participate in your hobbies and activities, you can deepen your bond and learn more about each other's passions and interests. So don't be afraid to share your interests and invite her to participate in the things that make you happy. Who knows, you might just discover a shared passion that can lead to a fulfilling and long-lasting relationship

"Invite her to dance"

Invite her to dance: Latinos love to dance and music is an important part of the culture. Invite her to dance and show off your skills on the dance floor.

Latinos love to dance, and music is a significant part of their culture. If you're interested in getting to know a Latina better, one way to break the ice is by asking her to dance. By doing so, you'll not only show your interest in her but also demonstrate your willingness to embrace her culture.

Dancing is an important social activity in Latino culture. It is a way to celebrate, express emotions, and connect with others. Latin dance styles are diverse and include salsa, merengue, bachata, cumbia, and reggaeton, to name a few. Each dance has its unique steps, rhythm, and cultural context, but they all share the same spirit of joy, passion, and rhythm.

If you want to invite a Latina to dance, you should do so with respect and confidence. Be polite and friendly, and make sure to ask her in a way that makes her feel comfortable and respected. If she agrees to dance with you, make sure to pay attention to her cues and follow her lead. Remember that dancing is a social activity, and the goal is to have fun and connect with your partner.

By inviting a Latina to dance, you'll not only show her your interest in her, but you'll also have the opportunity to learn more about her culture and experience the joy of dancing together. It's a great way to break the ice, build connections, and create lasting memories.

In conclusion, asking a Latina to dance is a great way to show your interest in her, connect with her culture, and have fun together. It's a social activity that allows you to break down barriers and build bridges between cultures. So next time you have the chance, go ahead and invite her to dance - you won't regret

cook together

Cook together: Food is an important part of Latin culture. Invite her to cook together and enjoy the food and company.

Cooking together is a wonderful way to bond with a Latina woman and share in the rich culinary traditions of her culture. Food is an essential part of the Latino culture, and by inviting her to cook with you, you can show her that you are interested in learning more about her heritage and sharing new experiences together.

To begin with, start by asking her what her favorite dish is and express your interest in learning how to make it. This will show her that you are interested in her and her culture, and that you want to share in the experience of preparing a meal together. Once you have decided on a dish to make, set aside some time to plan the menu and go shopping for the ingredients together. This will allow you to spend more time together and create a deeper connection.

When it comes time to cook, make sure to work as a team and assign tasks that each of you can handle. This will help to create a sense of teamwork and cooperation, and you will both have the opportunity to learn new cooking techniques and skills. As you cook together, take the time to share stories, memories, and experiences from your past. This will help to create a deeper connection between the two of you and will allow you to get to know each other on a more personal level.

Finally, as you sit down to enjoy your meal together, take the time to savor the flavors and aromas of the food, and the company of each other. By cooking and sharing a meal together, you will create memories that will last a lifetime and strengthen the bond between you.

In conclusion, cooking together is a great way to connect with a Latina woman, share in her culture, and create lasting memories together. By showing your interest in her heritage and learning new skills together, you can deepen your connection and build a strong foundation for a loving and lasting relationship.

Cooking together is an excellent way to bond with a Latina woman and share in the rich culinary traditions of her culture. Food is an essential part of the Latino culture, and by inviting her to cook with you, you can show her that you are interested in learning more about her heritage and sharing new experiences together.

To begin with, start by expressing your interest in cooking together and ask her what her favorite dish is. This will show her that you are genuinely interested in her and her culture and that you want to share in the experience of preparing a meal together. Once you have decided on a dish to make, set aside some time to plan the menu and go shopping for the ingredients together. This will allow you to spend more time together and create a deeper connection.

When it comes time to cook, make sure to work as a team and assign tasks that each of you can handle. This will help to create a sense of teamwork and cooperation, and you will both have the opportunity to learn new cooking techniques and skills. As you cook together, take the time to share stories, memories, and experiences from your past. This will help to create a deeper connection between the two of you and will allow you to get to know each other on a more personal level.

As you sit down to enjoy your meal together, take the time to savor the flavors and aromas of the food, and the company of each other. By cooking and sharing a meal together, you will create memories that will last a lifetime and strengthen the bond between you.

In conclusion, cooking together is a great way to connect with a Latina woman, share in her culture, and create lasting memories together. By showing your interest in her heritage and learning new skills together, you can deepen your connection and build a strong foundation for a loving and lasting relationship. So go ahead, invite her to cook with you, and enjoy the food and the company!

Be a good listener

Be a good listener: Listen carefully to what she has to say and show interest in her thoughts and feelings. Show her that you're interested in getting to know her on a deeper level.

Being a good listener means paying close attention to what the other person is saying and showing interest in their thoughts and feelings. It involves demonstrating that you are genuinely interested in getting to know them on a deeper level. Being a good listener is an essential aspect of building meaningful relationships, whether it be with friends, family, colleagues, or romantic partners.

One of the key components of being a good listener is active listening. This means focusing your attention solely on the person speaking and avoiding distractions such as your phone or other interruptions. It also involves using nonverbal cues such as maintaining eye contact, nodding your head, and giving verbal cues like "mm-hmm" or "I see" to indicate that you are engaged in the conversation.

Another important aspect of being a good listener is empathizing with the person speaking. This means putting yourself in their shoes and trying to understand their perspective, even if you don't necessarily agree with it. It also involves being patient and allowing the other person to express themselves fully without interrupting or offering unsolicited advice.

In addition to active listening and empathy, being a good listener also involves asking thoughtful questions and providing constructive feedback. This helps to demonstrate that you are genuinely interested in understanding the other person's thoughts and feelings and can help to facilitate a deeper and more meaningful conversation.

Overall, being a good listener is a crucial component of building strong and lasting relationships. By showing genuine interest in the thoughts and feelings of others and actively listening to their concerns, you can establish a deeper connection and foster a greater sense of trust and understanding.

In conclusion, being a good listener requires active listening, empathy, asking thoughtful questions, and providing constructive feedback. It's about showing genuine interest in the thoughts and feelings of others and building strong and meaningful relationships. By mastering the art of listening, you can become a more effective communicator and develop deeper connections with the people around you.

"Plan interesting dates"

Plan interesting dates: Plan interesting and creative dates that can showcase your personality and your likes. For example, you can go to a music festival, visit a museum, or go hiking together.

When it comes to dating, planning interesting and creative dates can be a great way to show off your personality and interests. By putting in the effort to plan a unique and exciting date, you can make a lasting impression and set the tone for a fun and enjoyable relationship.

One way to plan interesting dates is to think outside the box and consider activities that are not typically associated with traditional dating. For example, instead of just going out for dinner and a movie, you could plan a date to attend a music festival, visit a museum, or go on a hiking trip together.

Another important aspect of planning interesting dates is to consider the preferences and interests of your partner. This means taking the time to get to know them and finding activities that they will enjoy and appreciate. For example, if your partner is an art lover, you could plan a date to visit an art gallery or attend a painting class together.

In addition to being creative and tailored to your partner's interests, it's also important to be mindful of your budget when planning dates. This doesn't mean you have to spend a lot of money, but rather that you should find activities that fit within your budget and are still fun and engaging.

Overall, planning interesting and creative dates can be a great way to show off your personality, get to know your partner, and set the foundation for a fun and enjoyable relationship. By thinking outside the box, considering your partner's interests, and being mindful of your budget, you can plan dates that are both memorable and meaningful.

Be yourself

Be yourself: The most important thing is to be yourself and be honest about your feelings and thoughts. Show that you're interested in her as a person and that you value her culture and interests.

The idea behind (Be yourself) is to emphasize the importance of being authentic and honest about your thoughts and feelings when interacting with others. This is particularly relevant when trying to build a connection with someone from a different culture or background. To demonstrate your interest in the person and their culture, you can show curiosity and ask questions about their traditions, beliefs, and interests. Additionally, you can share your own experiences and perspectives in a respectful and open-minded way.

Be genuine and authentic: Avoid pretending to be someone you're not or adopting a persona that is not true to who you are.

Express interest: Show interest in the person you're interacting with by asking questions and actively listening to their responses.

Respect differences: Be open-minded and respectful of differences in culture, beliefs, and perspectives.

Share your own experiences: Share your own experiences and perspectives in a respectful and non-judgmental way.

Be honest about your feelings: If you're interested in someone, let them know in an honest and respectful way. If you're not interested, be honest and respectful in communicating that as well.

By following these instructions, you can demonstrate that you value the person and their culture, and build a genuine connection based on mutual respect and understanding.

Here are some recommendations for dressing appropriately for a date with a Latina woman, whether it's during the day or at night.

Daytime Dates:

1. Keep it Casual: For daytime dates, it's best to keep your attire casual yet stylish. You can't go wrong with a simple t-shirt or a button-down shirt paired with khaki or denim shorts. This outfit will keep you comfortable and cool during the day.

2. Comfortable Footwear: Since you'll likely be doing a lot of walking or other outdoor activities, you'll want to wear comfortable footwear. A pair of white sneakers or loafers would work well with this outfit.

3. Accessorize with Sunglasses: Don't forget to protect your eyes from the sun with a stylish pair of sunglasses. Not only will they add to your look, but they'll also provide necessary protection from UV rays.

4. Layer Up: Depending on the weather, you may want to bring a light jacket or a sweater to layer over your shirt. This will allow you to adjust your outfit as needed and keep you comfortable throughout the day.

Nighttime Dates:

1. Dress to Impress: For nighttime dates, you'll want to step up your game and dress to impress. A well-tailored suit or blazer paired with a dress shirt will make a strong impression and show your date that you take the occasion seriously.

2. Wear Dress Shoes: A pair of dress shoes will complete your nighttime look. Opt for a classic pair of oxfords or loafers in black or brown to match your suit or blazer.

3. Accessorize with a Watch: A stylish watch will not only complete your outfit but will also show your attention to detail. It's a great way to add a touch of elegance to your overall look.

4. Don't Forget the Cologne: Finally, don't forget to add a touch of your favorite cologne to complete your outfit. A good scent will leave a lasting impression and make you stand out from the crowd.

Weather Considerations:

1. Hot Weather: If you're going on a date in hot weather, it's essential to wear lightweight fabrics that allow your skin to breathe. Cotton and linen are great choices, and you should opt for lighter colors that reflect the sun's rays.

2. Cold Weather: If the weather is cold, you'll want to dress warmly. Layering is key, so make sure to wear a warm coat or jacket over your outfit. Don't forget to wear a scarf, hat, and gloves to keep your head and hands warm.

3. Rainy Weather: If it's raining, you'll want to wear waterproof shoes and a jacket with a hood to stay dry. You can also consider bringing an umbrella to stay dry while walking outside.

4. Windy Weather: If it's windy, you'll want to wear clothes that fit tightly to your body. Avoid loose-fitting clothing that could be blown around by the wind. You should also consider wearing a hat or cap to keep your hair from getting too messy.

In conclusion, dressing for a date with a Latina woman requires careful consideration of the weather, the occasion, and your personal style. By following these recommendations, you'll be sure to impress your date and make a lasting impression.

The use of a fragrance that matches (or is appropriate

Scientific Reasons:

1. Enhance Attractiveness: A study published in the International Journal of Cosmetic Science found that wearing a fragrance can enhance one's attractiveness and make them more appealing to potential partners. The researchers found that women are particularly sensitive to scent and that a pleasant fragrance can have a positive impact on their perception of a man's attractiveness.

2. Boost Confidence: Wearing a fragrance can also boost one's confidence and self-esteem. When you smell good, you feel good, and that confidence can be attractive to your date. Additionally, the scent of your fragrance can have a positive impact on your mood and make you feel more relaxed and at ease.

3. Create a Memorable Impression: Wearing a fragrance on a date can help create a memorable impression. When your date smells the fragrance on you, they will associate it with the positive experience of being with you, which can lead to a stronger emotional connection.

Cultural Reasons:

1. Personal Hygiene: In many Latin cultures, personal hygiene is highly valued, and smelling good is a sign of good grooming and self-care. Wearing a fragrance is considered an important aspect of personal hygiene, and many Latinas may view a man who doesn't wear a fragrance as lacking in this area.

2. Symbol of Masculinity: In Latin culture, masculinity is often associated with strength, confidence, and virility. Wearing a fragrance can be seen as a symbol of masculinity, as it signals that the man takes care of himself and pays attention to his appearance.

3. Traditional Gender Roles: In many Latin cultures, there are traditional gender roles that dictate how men and women should behave. Men are expected to be providers and protectors, while women are expected to be caretakers and nurturers. Wearing a fragrance can be seen as a way for men to fulfill their role as providers by investing in their personal grooming and appearance.

Choosing the Right Fragrance:

When choosing a fragrance for a date with a Latina woman, it's important to consider the time of day and the occasion. Here are some tips for choosing the right fragrance:

1. Daytime Dates: For daytime dates, it's best to wear a lighter fragrance that is not too overpowering. Fresh and citrusy scents are great options, as they are refreshing and energizing.

2. Nighttime Dates: For nighttime dates, you can wear a more intense fragrance that is warm and sensual. Woody and spicy scents are great options, as they are masculine and sophisticated.

3. Consider Your Date's Preferences: It's also important to consider your date's preferences when choosing a fragrance. If you know that your date likes a particular scent or brand, wearing it can be a great way to show that you pay attention to her likes and dislikes.

In conclusion, wearing a fragrance on a date with a Latina woman is important for both scientific and cultural reasons. By choosing the right fragrance and taking care of your personal grooming, you can create a memorable impression and show that you value personal hygiene and self-care.

to give a present"

Sure! If you want to give flowers and chocolates to a Latina woman to court her, there are a few things to keep in mind to avoid coming off as too over-the-top or excessive.

1. Choose the right flowers: In Latin culture, certain flowers are associated with specific meanings. For example, red roses signify love and passion, while yellow flowers can be seen as a sign of infidelity. Do a little research to make sure the flowers you choose convey the message you intend.

2. Keep it simple: You don't need to go overboard with the gifts to impress a Latina woman. A simple bouquet of flowers and a box of chocolates will suffice, especially if it's a first date or you're just getting to know each other.

3. Be genuine: It's important to be sincere in your gesture and express your feelings honestly. Don't give flowers and chocolates just because you think it's what you're supposed to do, but rather because you genuinely want to make her feel special.

So, to sum it up, keep it simple and sincere when giving flowers and chocolates to a Latina woman as a gift. Choose the right flowers and express your feelings honestly to avoid coming off as over-the-top or insincere.

Sure, here's an explanation of why you should avoid being too intense when courting a Latina woman:

Latina women are known for their fiery passion and zest for life, and it's understandable that you may be drawn to that energy. However, being too intense when courting a Latina woman can actually be a turnoff and could potentially harm your chances of developing a successful relationship.

One reason why being too intense can be problematic is that it can come across as insincere or inauthentic. When you're constantly bombarding a woman with intense displays of affection or attention, it can be difficult for her to tell whether you're genuinely interested in her or simply trying to impress her.

Additionally, Latina women often value independence and autonomy, and may feel uncomfortable or smothered by someone who is constantly trying to control or dominate the relationship. Being too intense can make it difficult for a woman to feel like she has the space and freedom to be herself in the relationship.

Finally, being too intense can simply be overwhelming for a woman, particularly if you're just getting to know each other. It's important to take the time to build a strong foundation of trust and communication before diving into intense displays of affection or devotion.

In summary, while it's natural to be drawn to a Latina woman's passion and energy, it's important to be mindful of not being too intense when courting her. This can come across as insincere, overwhelming, and may make her feel uncomfortable or smothered. Instead, take the time to build a strong foundation of trust and communication, and allow the relationship to develop naturally.

Sure, here's the continuation of the explanation:

It's important to remember that each woman is unique and has her own preferences when it comes to dating and relationships. However, in general, Latina women tend to appreciate men who are confident, respectful, and attentive without being overbearing.

Instead of being too intense, try to show your interest in her through thoughtful gestures and genuine conversations. For example, you could ask her about her interests and hobbies, and plan a date around an activity that she enjoys. Or, you could surprise her with a small gift or note that shows you were thinking about her.

It's also important to respect her boundaries and take things at a pace that feels comfortable for both of you. Don't push her to move faster than she's ready to, and be willing to listen to her if she expresses discomfort or concern.

Ultimately, the key to successfully courting a Latina woman is to be yourself and show her that you respect and appreciate her as an individual. Avoid being too intense or overbearing, and focus on building a connection based on trust, respect, and mutual interests. With patience and sincerity, you may be able to develop a meaningful and fulfilling relationship with a Latina woman.

www.ingramcontent.com/pod-product-compliance
Lightning Source LLC
Chambersburg PA
CBHW051934250726
48659CB00002B/997